oasis

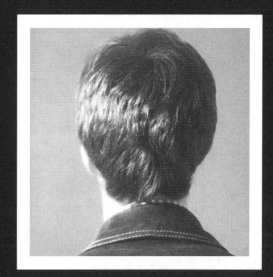

(WHAT'S THE STORY) MORNING GLORY ?

D1335958

WISE PUBLICATIONS
London / New York / Paris / Sydney / Copenhagen / Madrid

Exclusive Distributors:
Music Sales Limited
8/9 Frith Street, London W1V 5TZ, England.

Music Sales Pty Limited
120 Rothschild Avenue, Rosebery, NSW 2018, Australia.

Order No.AM934791
ISBN 0-7119-5464-X
This book © Copyright 1995 by Wise Publications.

Book design by Michael Bell Design.
Music arranged by Roger Day.
Music processed by Paul Ewers Music Design.

Printed and bound in Great Britain by
Caligraving Limited, Thetford, Norfolk.

(WHAT'S THE STORY) MORNING GLORY ?

Hello

Words & Music by Noel Gallagher

(includes extract from Hello, Hello, I'm Back Again - Words & Music by Gary Glitter & Mike Leander)

1. I don't feel as if I know you, you take up all my time.
(Verse 2 see block lyric)

The days are long and the nights will throw you a - way,

had the chance and threw it a - way_____ and it's nev - er gon - na be the same,__

_____ 'cause the years_____ are fol - low-ing by_____ like the rain,_____ it's

nev - er gon - na be the same_____ till the life_____ I knew_____ comes to my__

1.

_____ house and says_____ hel - lo._____

Verse 2:
There ain't no sense in feeling lonely
They got no faith in you
Well I've got a feeling you still owe me
So wipe the shit from your shoes.

Don't Look Back In Anger

Words & Music by Noel Gallagher

1. Slip in - side— the eye of your mind,— don't you know you might— find—
(Verse 2 see block lyric)

a bet - ter place to play.—

bloom, stand up be - side the fi - re - place,

take that look from off your face, you ain't ev - er gon - na burn my

heart out.

Vocal each time

So Sal - ly can wait she knows it's too late as {we're / she's} walk - ing on by

11

Verse 2:
Take me to the place where you go
Where nobody knows if it's night or day
Please don't put your life in the hands
Of a rock 'n' roll band who'll throw it all away.

I'm gonna start a revolution from my head
'Cause you said the brains I had went to my head
Step outside, the summertime's in bloom
Stand up beside the fireplace, take that look from off your face
'Cause you ain't never gonna burn my heart out.

Roll With It

Words & Music by Noel Gallagher

say what you say, don't let a-ny-bo-dy get in your way— 'cause it's all— too much—

— for me to take.— Don't ev - er

(D.%. instrumental)

stand a - side,— don't ev - er be de - nied,— if you wan - na

be who you'd be if you're com - in' with me.— I

think I've got a feel-in' I've lost____ in - side;____ I think I'm gon - na take me a - way____

____ and____ hide.____ I'm think-ing of things____ that I____ just can't____ a - bide.____

(Vocal both times)

I know the roads____ down which____

____ your life____ will drive.____ I

find the key____ that lets____ you slip____ in - side.____

Kiss the girl,____ she's not____ be - hind____ the door.__

You know, I think I re - cog - nise____ ____ your face,____ but I've ne - ver seen you be - fore.____

be de - nied,— if you wan - na be who you'd be if you're com-in' with me.— I

C   **G/B**   **A7sus4**

Play 8 times

think I've got a feel - ing I've lost_____ in - side.— (I)

C   **G/B**   **A7sus4**   **C**   **G/B**   **A7sus4**

C   **G/B**   **A7sus4**   **G**

Wonderwall

Words & Music by Noel Gallagher

To - day is gon - na be the day that they're gon - na throw it back to you,—

by now you should- 've some - how re - al - ised what you got - ta do.—

I don't be-lieve__ that an - y - bo - dy feels the way I do__ a - bout you now.__

1. Back-beat the word was on the street that the fi - re in your heart is out.__
(Verse 2 see block lyric)

I'm sure you've heard it all be-fore but you nev-er real-ly had a doubt.__

There are ma - ny things— that I—— would like to say to you— but I don't know how,—

{be - cause / I said}

may - be— you're gon - na be the one that

saves me,— and af - ter all——

Verse 2:
Today was gonna be the day
But they'll never throw it back to you
By now you should've somehow
Realised what you're not to do
I don't believe that anybody
Feels the way I do
About you now.

And all the roads that lead you there were winding
And all the lights that light the way are blinding
There are many things that I would like to say to you
But I don't know how.

Hey Now

Words & Music by Noel Gallagher

1. 3. I hitched a ride with my soul by the
(Verse 2 see block lyric)

side of the road,___ just as the sky___ turned black.___

I took a walk with my fame down me-mo-ry lane,— I never did find— my way back.— You know that I got-ta say, time's slip-ping a-way,— I what will it hold— for me?— What am I gon-na do while I'm

'cause time's__ no chain,__ feel__ no shame.__

2. The

Feel___ no shame___

Verse 2:
The first thing I saw
As I walked through the door
Was a sign on the wall that read
It said you might never know
That I want you to know
What's written inside of your head

And time as it stands
Won't be held in my hands
Or living inside of my skin
And as it fell from the sky
I asked myself why
Can I never let anyone in?

The Swamp Song

Words & Music by Noel Gallagher

Some Might Say

Words & Music by Noel Gallagher

1. Some might say that sun-shine fol-lows thun-der
(Verse 2 see block lyric)

go and tell it to the man who can-not shine.

Some might say that

gain.

The sink is full of fish - es 'cause

she's got dir - ty dish - es on the brain.

[It was

ov - er - flow - ing gent - ly but it's all e - le - men - tary my

And my dog's been itch - ing, itch - ing in the kitch - en once a -

1.

friend.
gain.

Verse 2:
Some might say they don't believe in heaven
Go and tell it to the man who lives in hell
Some might say you get what you've been given
If you don't get yours I won't get mine as well.

Cast No Shadow

Words & Music by Noel Gallagher

Here's a thought for ev-'ry man who tries to un-der-stand what is in his hands.

He

walks a - long— the o - pen road— of love— and life,— sur - viv - ing if he can.—

Bound with all the weight— of all— the words— he tried to say,—

chained to all— the pla - ces that— he ne - ver wished— to stay.—

they stole his pride.

As they took his soul they stole his pride.

1.

As he faced the sun he cast

no sha-dow.

She's Electric

Words & Music by Noel Gallagher

1. She's e-lec-tric, she's in a fa-mi-ly full of ec-cen-
(Verse 2 see block lyric)

-trics, she's done things I ne-ver ex-pec-ted and I

need more time.— She's— got a sis-

-ter and God on-ly knows— how I've missed— her, and on the

palm of her hand— is a blis-ter and I need more time.—

Can I be e-lec-tric too? Ah ah.

Verse 2:
She's got a brother
We don't get on with one another
But I quite fancy her mother
And I think that she likes me
She's got a cousin
In fact she's got 'bout a dozen
She's got one in the oven
But it's nothing to do with me.

Morning Glory

Words & Music by Noel Gallagher

need a lit-tle time to wake— up wake— up, need a lit-tle time to wake—

— up, need a lit-tle time to rest— your mind,— you

know you should— so I guess— you might— as well.—

What's the sto-ry morn-ing glo-ry, well,—

you need a lit - tle time to wake— up, wake— up,

well,— what's the sto - ry morn -

- ing glo - ry, well,— you

1.

need a lit - tle time to wake— up, wake— up.

Verse 2:
All your dreams are made
When you're chained to the mirror with your razor blade
Today's the day that all the world will see
Another sunny afternoon
I'm walking to the sound of my favourite tune
Tomorrow doesn't know what it doesn't know too soon.

The Swamp Song

Words & Music by Noel Gallagher

Champagne Supernova

Words & Music by Noel Gallagher

slow-ly walk-ing down the hall fast-er than a can-non ball,

where were you while we were get-ting high. Some day you will

find me caught be-neath the land - slide, in a cham-

- pagne su-per-no - va in the sky. Some day you will find me caught be-neath the land-

slide,_____ in a cham-pagne su-per-no-va, a

cham-pagne su-per-no-va in the sky._____

1. Wake up the dawn and ask— her why,— a
(Verse 2 see block lyric)

dream-er dreams_ she ne-ver dies,— wipe that tear a-way— now from your eyes..

How ma-ny spe-cial peo-ple change— how ma-ny lives are liv-ing strange,—

Repeat ad lib. to fade

Verse 2:
How many special people change
How many lives are living strange
Where were you while we were getting high?
Slowly walking down the hall
Faster than a cannon ball
Where were you while we were getting high?